OLD SAYINGS I JUST MADE UP

by Professor Ray Grant

OLD SAYINGS I JUST MADE UP

PROFESSOR RAY GRANT

All rights reserved.

Copyright © 2015

No part of this book may be reproduced or transmitted in any form or by any means, electronic or mechanical, including photocopying, recording, or by any information storage and retrieval system, without permission in writing from the publisher.

For information address:

Professor Ray Grant
ProfessorRayGrant@gmail.com

Twitter @ProfRayGrant

to

Paula, my wife, who taught me love.
And to my children, Rae and Donovan,
who taught me patience and joy. And to
all of my students, they kept me
thinking.

1. When you leave a situation and others have chosen to remain, most will say you've quit but really you're just continuing your journey without them.

2. People are always looking for their moment to shine instead of shining in every moment.

3. You can't stop yourself and others from dying but you can stop yourself and others from living.

4. What's beneath the surface of love is the least attractive but is the most valuable yet it is what we avoid the most.

5. The meaning of "family and friends" does not mean "these are the people I can safely misuse and abuse."

6. I've actually heard people say, "Had I known you were going to make it, I would've supported you" or "I would've supported you more."

7. It takes a team to beat a team.

8. When you need money, people give you advice. When you need advice, people want your money.

9. As rare as it is to find a good friend, it's just as rare to be one.

10. Don't take old baggage on new adventures.

11. So called "great communicators" rarely hear a word you're saying.

12. You are always judged by the company you keep especially when you're alone.

13. When we detect freedom in another, it frightens us because we don't know how to be free. We want to pull that person back to where we are held captive.

14. If you don't want criticism then don't desire attention.

15. The more great things you desire in life the more you have to say goodbye to bad habits.

16. You cannot inspire those full of fear. You can only train them in the way of success until they someday realize they can achieve.

17. This society was not designed to provide happiness for you. It was designed for you to obey the design.

18. Being a parent is more importantly not about being a better parent but it is more about being a better you.

19. If you don't allow your children to fail around you, they'll just fail around someone else.

20. If we look at giving our love to another as a sacrifice, it's not love at all. It's a favor.

21. Unsuccessful people actually know the secret to success. They just apply it to things that aren't important.

22. Smart people know what they want and know how to get it. Intelligent people know what others want and know how to get it for them. Brilliant people are smart and intelligent.

23. I know you by the way you treat others you claim to love.

24. Living for someone else's happiness is like living for someone else's bed to be made. That person is just going to mess it up again.

25. I've had people contact me from my past and say to me, "I used to not like you." I ask "Why?" They'll say, "Because back then you didn't have anything but you were still so honest and confident and I hated that about you." Well, you're really not going to

like me now. So why are you contacting me?

26. I have noticed that most people don't negotiate salaries. We generally accept the first offer then work really hard trying to impress our employer enough to be granted a raise. We are always shocked when we discover the new person hired is making more money. That new person more than likely negotiated a higher salary. It wasn't personal in that case. You have to be willing to say "No." It's mainly about understanding the salary range of the position. Your experience and value is evident in the first offer. How far to

the extreme is another thing. If you make premium going in, there's no room for a raise except with the normal cost of living raise. Many take the max and have to leave that job or change title or position in a few years. Or you'll be forced out by a new person willing to take less money.

27. Think of all of the good people you've overlooked in your life. They weren't good salespeople. The bad ones were great salespeople.

28. What destroys relationships is when one or the other person has an

interesting life prior to getting involved. The energy they normally put into their interests will be transferred to the new person. It's interesting at first but then over time that person will find this new person is actually less interesting than their old way of living.

29. Impatience keeps relationships off balance. What keeps you from impatience is the belief in yourself not others. You can't dream for others. They have their own ideas of themselves. Get out of others what they're willing to give. What you force out of them will leave a bitter taste to your self-satisfaction. If you feel you

can do better than this particular relationship then move on and find someone else that will live up to your expectations. But chances are you'll be right back where you were in your last relationship because it's really all about you and your impatience.

30. When you come from little or nothing, others will try to hold you to that.

31. The truth and your experiences are two different things. How do you know you weren't lied to while experiencing your truth?

32. Poor kids protect what little they have. When poor and privileged kids interact, the privileged and poor are protecting totally different things.

33. Most judge and criticize you according to the perfection in their minds because they have not come to grips with their own imperfections.

34. When most find perfection, we have a tendency to ruin it looking for perfect perfection.

35. Those that are lucky profess competence and skill.

36. I have to say negative things about negative influences in order to see the positive things.

37. If you have shortcomings, don't let your children know because they'll think they have those same shortcomings.

38. Sometimes settling is not a bad thing. Sometimes settling is realistic. Some people and things we just can't afford.

39. Sometimes the help others need is simply just getting out of their way.

40. Chasing dreams: young people know what's valuable to them; however, sometimes they don't know what is valuable. You have to slowly introduce them to what is valuable as opposed to what is popular and most times valueless. There has to be a rewards system or else it will be difficult

when they see other young people "having fun" while the dream chasers toil away at their distant reward. Consequences, I see as punishment. Sometimes it's best to be naive when approaching a dream. Reality can sometimes deter a journey. There must be plenty of pep talk and motivation available at all times and it must be inspiring.

41. I have noticed that my son has been conditioned to make decisions based on his thoughts only. On the other hand, my daughter has been conditioned to make decisions based on her thoughts and feelings.

42. Instead of life propelling most people forward, life actually paralyzes them.

43. If you are gifted or talented enough, eventually you won't have to ask others to accommodate you. They will volunteer or be forced by others.

44. Our biggest problems occur when we try to recreate something that already exists when what we should do is simply copy it.

45. Understand the next level and you will grow.

46. Every noise in the dark is not someone trying to kill you.

47. Every concern a friend or loved one has is not important enough to drop everything you're doing.

48. My son is being conditioned to serve and share with his future girlfriend/wife. However, these girls are

being conditioned to not serve a boyfriend/husband or share. She's being taught to be independent. I may have to rethink my son's relationship conditioning.

49. Success is not obvious until afterwards.

50. Stormy personalities think the whole world is storming.

51. Sometimes children don't need your help. They only need your approval or disapproval.

52. People that aren't accustomed to thinking, when they finally do think, they think themselves into a bunch of trouble.

53. I don't need your opinion. I have my own. I need facts and your expertise.

54. I've realized another significant role I have as a husband and father, I demand that the children respect their mother.

55. You can plan and prepare all you want but you still need luck. You can make your own luck but you still gotta be lucky.

56. Some people are only great conversationalists when they're being phony.

57. Most people don't know how to help you because you haven't decided what kind of help you will accept and they don't know what you will appreciate.

58. I know people that have so much going for themselves but choose to be miserable because it's what they're used to.

59. You ask what makes me angry so you'll know what to avoid saying or doing around me. Simple, they are the same things you don't like said and done to and around you.

60. Be careful with the cute lies you tell and magical illusion secrets you never reveal to children, most engrain and actually make them a part of their adult rationalizations.

61. Great ideas and motivation most times come from socializing/conversations with brilliant people.

62. There's a difference between luck and genius. Genius can duplicate excellence at will.

63. So many won't take the steady workable reality. They'll throw that away for the fantasy that someday awaits them.

64. I meet creative people with great instincts but their lack of intelligence gets in their way.

65. Salespeople try to convince me that the best deal for me is also the best deal for them. No, the best deal for me is not the best deal for them.

66. The more difficult "growing pain" situations you're saved from by others or you "save" others from experiencing, the more difficult it will be later in life when there's no one around willing to help.

67. If you are unable to recognize an opportunity when it presents itself, it may go away as if it never existed.

68. Classless people are constantly skeptical of those that are classy. They think their behavior is phony too.

69. People are always throwing their ill-prepared children into the mix with well-prepared children expecting them to not only compete but win.

70. There's more truth on the comedy stage than in the pulpit.

71. Don't be old with regrets about sex, romance or lust. I think if you see what you want you should go after it. You only live once. It's just being human. Don't be dehumanized by societal

standards. You'll be the only one in your grave or urn.

72. Now that you've been let go by your company, don't say what you did while with that company; say what you can do without it.

73. If you are not happy then change your concept of happiness.

74. I only reveal what I know works. If you dismiss it, it tells me more about you.

75. People are reluctant to share their happiness but will quickly share their unhappiness and even swap their unhappiness for your happiness.

76. Frustration occurs when non-thinkers try to think for thinkers.

77. You can't follow people without knowing their honest reasoning behind what they do and what got them to that point in their lives.

78. If you want to really understand life, watch a sporting game. The better coaches are always trying to lobby and influence the refs with their interpretation of the rules to get an advantage for their team and against the other team. If you don't have someone lobbying for you in life, chances are the rules will be in favor of those with better coaches.

79. People, society will always remain flawed because each child born will yearn to live the lies history has told.

80. Be careful letting everyone know you're the smartest one in the room. They will bore you with nonsense.

81. As soon as you think you know the answer, the question changes.

82. Feel your way through life only after you've thought your way to this point.

83. People believe because they volunteer to do for you, that you're

obligated to volunteer and do the same for them, when they think you should.

84. Free yourself of temperament. Feeling comes from motion which leads to emotion.

85. Stars are stars and average people are not. Stars can't afford to (as much as they would like) behave like average people. The fall for a star is farther and harder.

86. The better person has the ability to adjust. Don't be so quick to replace or substitute that kind of person for one that can't adjust.

87. No matter how good you are or your presentation is, people that can't help you will always ask, "You got something else?"

88. You're just on a "things to do" list in another person's life. And that person is on your list.

89. When you're talented, others immediately want to place you into a category of something they've seen before.

90. I was asked about emotions needed to make music. There's no emotion in nature and it sounds and feels beautiful.

91. We only imitate nature. That's how music began. We heard the birds chirp. They're not emotional. They're surviving.

92. People actually believe their self-importance, believing they're tolerating you until you dismiss them.

93. I've been on stage thousands of times. The first times I was so emotional. After a while I learned how to make people feel without including my feelings. I'd have never lasted if I had kept up that emotional pace. Fake it until you make it but also make it until you know how to fake it.

94. When creating, use your brains, sight, touch, sense of smell and hearing not just your heart. You're limiting

yourself. If I make people feel differently, I have them for that moment. If I can make people think differently, I have them forever.

95. When talking innovation, most people will take the conversation to the safe zone to avoid thinking or changing their lifestyles.

96. Life is like you're butt naked in a jungle trying to fight everything with a gun. But what about mosquitoes?

97. Instead of fighting nature, imitate it. That's what the first people on the planet did. There are new ideas everywhere. They're limitless. Tap into it.

98. I can go without doubt. Doubt is just an opinion. Failure is a fact. Criticism is an objective if coming from the right qualified individuals but still that's opinion. I don't accept failure. That happens when you quit.

99. We awaken every morning faced with the weaknesses we fell asleep

with. Then spend that day fighting the temptation of those weaknesses again.

100. People try to limit you with their own limitations. I cannot limit you with my limitations as I can't allow you to limit me with yours.

101. If you outgrow me, you were too advanced for me in the 1st place. If I outgrow you, I can't continue to listen to the same old complaints.

102. You can't give others confidence. You can only take it away. How one receives confidence may not be the way you know how to give it. Therefore, you may not be the right person to lead everybody.

103. Musicians and artists are chasing the dollar instead of innovating the next phase of their art. In the day of reality shows, we are now in the phase of reality art.

104. If you introduce greatness to people, they will first marvel and admire it. But if you constantly

introduce greatness to them, they will begin to knit-pick and criticize it eventually running greatness away and be left with the mediocrity they were once used to.

105. Don't let others convince you that your happiness is actually unhappiness.

106. People want to charge you an amount of money based on what they think you can afford rather than what their service is worth.

107. People in positions of authority over you or gatekeepers that treat you disrespectfully or indifferently, when you surpass them, they want you to continue to treat them with respect because they were established before you.

108. Most people don't know how to make others happy because their own happiness depends on others – kind of like a corporation not being able to make its employees wealthy because the corporation's wealth depends on the employees' labor.

109. If you use force of will or good looks to get what you want, unless you are shrewd in business, the twilight of your life will be dim.

110. Many of us never take time to find out what others already know or don't know before we begin teaching.

111. I know so many people that try to impress others that care nothing about them and take for granted those that actually care about them.

112. Whenever a super-talent is spotted, whatever got that super-talent to that point is usually eliminated by thieves.

113. I get it now. Parents are afraid to discipline their children, afraid their children won't love them.

114. If you try to prove a dumb person is smart while the dumb person is intent on proving you wrong, the dumb person will win every time.

115. Many artists believe their art is not viable unless they scar it with ugliness that reminds them of where they're from or wish to be.

116. Most people hit rock bottom before they can hear their truth.

117. I just broke away mentally and emotionally from the jaws of creativity death. Creativity death is others expectations of what I do. I used to hold stock in that until I realized most people's goals are other people's goals. They want the benefits of the grind. They don't want the grind.

118. Many times when we judge, we're setting ourselves up to be judged based on our logic, critique and refinement of taste.

119. If you're lucky enough to meet someone with great ideas, STHU and listen.

120. Most of us fail simple tasks because we assume the solutions are beyond us when a mentor could solve our dilemmas in seconds.

121. Many above average children fight to be average or below average just so they can fit in.

122. Those that make mistakes, learn from them, take responsibility for them and try not to continuously spread the pain.

123. This dude I know seems to know everything about business except people. He explains the ways to success then all of the possible pitfalls which makes people spend too much time

worrying about the pitfalls, paralyzing everyone.

124. We picture perfect success in our heads but we most times fail to picture the perfect steps it takes to reach that perfect success.

125. It's expensive to be phony especially for those that support phony people.

126. Most times successful people won't help you because they're afraid

they'll lose you as a good employee, friend, admirer or flunky.

127. I introduced two self-proclaimed professionals to one another. One treated the other like an amateur. Now I know who the real professional is.

128. It's difficult to get others to support what you're doing if the person sleeping next to you doesn't.

129. People think because they heard or read something about a subject once, it must be true.

130. Be careful not to become too bored with success too quickly. Failure is an exciting hole very difficult to dig yourself out of.

131. Being raised in negative environments for so long, it is difficult to understand positive people who don't see negative points of view. Being raised in a positive, nurturing environment, you can detect negativity immediately.

132. Don't push the people that actually care about you past the "I don't care about you anymore" point.

133. If you speak to an unsuccessful person about pretty much anything, you'll quickly discover why that person is unsuccessful.

134. No matter how wonderful you are or how great you do something, classless people will grow tired of it. They push you to be something or do

something else. They either destroy you or push you away.

135. We often fail because we believe the obvious things can't be that simple.

136. Most people don't want real answers or solutions. They only want dialogue, to be heard.

137. When you have a consistent money maker, no matter how little money it's making, it's making money. Don't listen to criticism.

138. You're not exclusive to problems. Everybody has them. Some accept and deal with them better. If you can fix them, do it. If you can't, there's nothing you can do.

139. People believe that not spending money is being negative, going into debt for temporary pleasure is a good enough reason.

140. I taught college for 20 years and learned that no matter what a child's socioeconomic background, the teacher

has to demand respect from day one. That is what all kids expect from their teachers and coaches. If the teacher or coach doesn't command respect, the student will cease to give it. New teachers in training are not faced with the proper challenges. Unfortunately, like many jobs and professions, you learn as you go. If a teacher is a quick study, he or she will do well. Most times, educating students is nurturing. However, love is not a requirement. The teacher's job is to make the students better students only if the students are willing. I could care less if my child's teacher loves him or not. That is not the teacher's job. I have to constantly get on my son about giving his teachers respect, warranted to them or not.

141. People have the hardest time accepting that others close to them or others they have authority over don't have the same beliefs.

142. When I travel to other countries and learn of the superstitions and various customs, they appear strange. However, if I were taught those same things by my parents, relatives, neighbors, teachers and politicians, I too would probably believe those things.

143. It's the masses that need the uplifting. Many of us that find some success move away from the masses, most times the successful have to for various reasons. But until the masses consciously elevate, the few successful will be bound to the acceptance of degradation that the masses don't have the resources alone to overcome.

144. My fight is your fight when there's an injustice happening against you not when there's simply a difference against your opinions or beliefs.

145. So few can find truth because we're not conditioned to accept it.

146. We become so consumed by what we want, most times we neglect what we need.

147. It is so painful when family or close friends worship the words of strangers over yours then are later hurt by the stranger's deception.

148. If you're in a hole and broke, why are you celebrating? That's how you got into the predicament you're in.

149. Some actually believe by holding back information, it's going to make everything workout. No. It makes simple things worse.

150. Certain people you cannot include in your planning. They will kill your plans and birth their own.

151. I used to think most people were going around looking for approval but are really looking for disapproval. Ten people can be encouraging but let one person be negative and that's all they need to quit.

152. Too many people want their success to be exciting. That's why they'll never reach it. The excitement is in reflection.

153. It's tough navigating through life with your feelings. How things work have no feelings.

154. If your methods have failed you and you meet a successful mentor that helps you succeed, why suddenly revert back to your old ways?

155. You can rarely talk others through future trouble. They have to already be in it. You can't will your experience to others. They have to live their own life in order to learn.

156. Old people should get together and write a book called "The Stuff In Life That Ain't' Important." And it

should be mandatory reading for anybody under 70.

157. Most people believe there's a better offer coming so they pass on the first good one. But in life there's usually only that one good offer.

158. A temporary way of getting by to make a living most times becomes a way of life.

159. We fail when we spend time and energy on insignificant things leaving us

confused or too exhausted to complete the important tasks. We should be actually building the house but we're at the paint store deciding what color to paint the basement bathroom that hasn't even been built yet.

160. A lot of times we tell children they're "the best" without making them prove it. They become adults that get angry when others want proof.

161. To be a leader of people, you really don't have to understand yourself. You have to understand

people. Understanding yourself is a bonus.

162. Most people aren't looking for answers. They're looking for audiences.

163. I know people that constantly struggle with unnecessary things, things they can Google and get the answers.

164. I have the hardest time trying to describe happiness to others until they finally realize they're actually in a good

place. But after a while they're unhappy again.

165. Usually, we already have what we need but we can't see it. Those things we can't see probably weren't meant for us to have because we are blinded by something unimportant in the scheme of things.

166. We spend so much time making others feel special on little things that we have no extra time and energy to help others thrive.

167. It doesn't matter how well you treat a person, if the loving intent is not behind your generosity, most people won't like or respect you. On the other hand, if you do nothing for anybody but you show compassion and loving intent behind your doing nothing for them, people will love you.

168. Most people are on a quest for unhappiness and you can't stop them. You can't change their minds. They're relentless. So get out of their way before you get trampled and become a casualty.

169. If you say "No" enough times for others to leave you alone, others will eventually get the hint and you will be alone.

170. Happiness to most means selfishness.

171. When I hear a coach say a very good player is not coachable, chances are they mean they're not good enough to coach this kid.

172. You cannot be an optimist with those that are trying to hurt you. Defend yourself and others around you or else suffer the consequences.

173. Underachievement and stupidity looks like fun to children and most adults.

174. Many of us are constantly favored with plenty of opportunities but we aren't conditioned to recognize them as opportunities. Most times we just see opportunities as inconveniences too different than what we're used to in order to take advantage of them.

175. In relationships, do for others what they can't easily do for themselves. That's what makes you special. Otherwise, you make yourself easily expendable, and it's better for the other person to be alone.

176. Most people want to get better but by doing more of the same. They want to get better and keep the same bad habits.

177. Even cold, heartless people want to be charmed.

178. Don't be too confident that you overlook others' insecurities or needs. You need them to help support your confidence.

179. If you don't upgrade your life when it's time, you'll only be frustrated later when others have passed you by.

180. Don't ask for advice, we discuss it and you go off and do something different and fail then you ask me to repeat what I said.

181. Equality is not a privilege; it's a right. However, all individuals should not be treated or deserve to be treated equally when they are not humble, intelligent or gracious enough to give others that same right.

182. In relationships, people want to be treated special on the occasions everyone else is being treated special, ie. holidays, birthdays, anniversaries... And they want to be treated special on days when no one else is being treated special, ie. Sunday thru Sat. That's too much.

183. Most of us are trained to be amateurs. Pros are trained the same but are taught to cheat if need be.

184. Before two people get into a relationship, they should make a list of things that the other person can do to make the other happy. If you have a long list or if the items are constantly changing, you should probably remain single and spare the other person.

185. What are you going to do when the plan breaks down? Which most

plans do. The person who knows what to do then is the leader.

186. When you're on your deathbed, what will you probably remember about your life? Then while you're alive and able, those are the things you should try to accomplish now.

187. I used to believe the dream would come save me not realizing the dream was inside of me.

188. Emotion moves people. Facts freeze them.

189. Most people only know how to live from one awkward moment to next. That is where they feel most comfortable.

190. If you dream big, just live your dream. Don't expect others to live your dream too. They have their own dreams.

191. Beware of the coward that is only brave around you. The coward is attracted to your independence and strength. The coward is looking for acceptance from you. Once the coward gets acceptance from you, the coward will then try to convert you into cowardice.

192. Being mature or being true to oneself is when you allow others to be themselves around you and be able to check them when being themselves is negatively affecting you.

193. When you keep your problems to yourself, that affects your relationships and creates new problems you don't intend to create.

194. Freedom allows improvisation. Slavery forces ingenuity.

195. You can dazzle most with clichés. It's like selling fool's gold. But you can't buy anything with it.

196. Most people care more about their image and the perception others

have of them more than they do their actual realities.

197. Love was taught to us. And like everything else, how you view love depends on your teachers.

198. You can be considered perfect by someone until you become too close; then they begin to find fault in you either because they want you for themselves but can't have you or they want you for themselves but are afraid they're not good enough to keep you so they try to convince you "you're not all that."

199. The entire world of people moves on opinion. The natural universe moves on fact.

200. Once a lie is revealed anything established after that may not be valid even if the results are positive.

201. Most people make a whole lot of sense until pressure is on them then nothing they say makes any sense.

202. People fight for control to make the decisions and most are wrong. Afterwards, they want forgiveness and to continue making the decisions.

203. If anyone has a goal and can't get there on their own without someone else's direction, that person needs a leader. If that person can reach their goal on their own but would rather have company on their journey, that's companionship.

204. There are so many bad teachers. They think giving kids more or less will

make them better. No, inspire them and they can achieve anything.

205. I know people that are absolutely brilliant... but not when it counts.

206. People want to argue their opinions with you then ask you not to cite your credentials because they have none.

207. Sometimes you have to ask others what's important to them so as not to

waste time. And most times you'll find they don't know what's important.

208. No matter what, you have to be yourself, not who others want you to be... because in hard times you will be alone. And when you're alone, be alone with the happy you not the you others wanted you to be.

209. You cannot base your truth solely on your own personal experiences especially if other people are involved. They have different perspectives of the same truth. That's why we have judges

because there's always another side to the truth.

210. You have to continuously motivate others to love you. It doesn't have to be much. It can be small gestures like giving others your time or some time alone.

211. Taking righteousness to the grave is just not righteous. It should be left behind. Take the negativity with you to your grave.

212. I can't be around scary people too long. After a while, they'll convince you to be afraid of everything they're afraid of. Now both of y'all scared.

213. The success of rejection is success.

214. Most people believe you need their approval before you can consider yourself successful or worthy of success.

215. You're looking to make a point rather than make a truth.

216. Some people are dream killers but actually believe they are there to spare dreamers from disappointment.

217. People desperately try to fit others into their plans. They are so arrogant, naive or selfish to believe their plans and ideas are best.

218. Most people's happiness is like their feelings. It changes.

219. People will argue against a good thing that works only because they don't understand it, they've never seen it before, or they didn't think of it first.

220. It bothers me to see parents knowingly place their children in environments and situations that are detrimental to their development, watch the kids lose confidence, take them out, get their confidence rebuilt, then place them right back into that same environment. That's like placing your kids in a cage of wild animals, take them out, patch and stitch them up then place them right back into the cage. Then say, "They have to learn

sometimes." What is that lesson? No, that's saying to the kids, "Don't trust the person placing you back into that cage of wild animals." Now, if it's a matter of pure economics that a family is in that predicament then that's just an unfortunate case of circumstance.

221. Nature never thinks it's crazy. That's a people concept.

222. A young mind cannot be intellectually stimulated without allowing the young person to live a little. And on the contrary, you cannot have a young person only live without

exercise in thinking. Or that person will never development into a complete human being.

223. In business, if you put people together too soon, they have a tendency to go off on tangents and the business never gets done.

224. In a business dealing, what appears to be a rip off to one may actually be a great deal for another. Experience and intelligence makes all the difference.

225. The expectations are rarely the realities. Either we underestimate others or overestimate our own abilities.

226. Art is making others believe your truth or your lie.

227. There are people that support and love you only when you're struggling. Once you make it, they actually dislike you.

228. I want to know the truth up front. People want to get you involved emotionally or financially before they reveal to you or you discover the truth for yourself.

229. Most people can only be happy for you if you're struggling without them.

230. Most people want you to come into their lives and get comfortable. They never offer to come into your life and find comfort.

231. Don't ask me to look at and understand the negativity. Look at and understand the positivity.

232. People less happy than you will try to convince you that your happiness is a fraud - that you have to see life or circumstances from their perspective to see how unhappy you really are or should be.

233. When the universe places your wishes into play, most people panic and rush them, stop them or try to manipulate them until those wishes ultimately fail.

234. You can tell those that won't be able to handle success by how they treat those that are not successful.

234. Keep your word to yourself. I'll take your action.

235. I observe insecure people that purposely start fights with secure people expecting the secure not to retaliate and take it easy on them because they feel the secure should be strong enough to take it.

236. Please your audience not your critics.

237. Maybe they love what you can do for them but don't care for the messenger. I apologize to no one for what I know works for me.

238. When we say "Sorry, I wasn't thinking" after we make a simple mistake. Does that mean we turn our thinking on and off like a faucet?

239. Those that talk all the time, if you want to shut them up, tell them to show you what they've done.

240. The only way to deal with another's unrealistic fantasies is to take away their basic freedom. Over time their expectations will diminish and they'll begin to appreciate what they used to take for granted.

241. If you're not being protected or carried by others, natural selection is still in full effect.

242. If you try to please others during your process to achieve, you'll never accomplish your goals. You have to first complete your process without interference and deal with the results. That's the chance you take if you want to be successful.

243. I am not responsible for your excuses.

244. People think like this: "Don't punish me and hold me to the things I mess up or get wrong. Admire, praise and reward me for my good intentions and for what I meant to do right."

245. I think sometimes it's best to keep people needing you especially when it comes to money because they respect the money and the fact you have it.

246. Most people have so much fear in them they won't fight important fights or break any man made laws. They will rebel in subtle ways by not following societal simple rules and unwritten rules that allow people to function together in harmony.

247. People always want to jump on board after all of the hard work and sacrifice has been done. They want to help manage you then. I've actually had someone say to me, "Call me when you've made it. I'll come work with you then!"

248. Some people actually believe their children are more important to you than your own kids are to you.

249. When you meet someone that will do anything for you, don't kill their spirit by being picky.

250. There's nothing wrong with your ideas being wrong. People will avoid revealing their bad ideas but will show their bad actions. Why not get help with your ideas first instead of seeking help after your actions have failed?

251. Don't accuse others of trying to make you look bad because they're excelling and you're lazy.

252. With most people you have to play detective before you make a move or a run with them. Whatever craziness

is in their lives will affect you too. If you question them and they become upset, nervous or nonchalant with their answer be suspicious, double-check.

253. Too many people wait for perfection and waste too much time. Perfection requires luck and you can't depend on luck. You have to get in there, fail and learn from it then get back in there, fail and learn from that. You fail your way up.

254. Those that don't have success believe they know more than those that do. They just think they have bad luck.

255. If you come up with a new idea or concept, those that attack it or you because it's new are indoctrinated and are only acting out on their fear and bad training.

256. Check yourself, if the first words that come out of your mouth are always associated with fear, negativity or indifference.

257. Don't get in people's ears bragging about somebody or something that's mediocre. You're telling on yourself.

258. People get to a certain level of thinking and shut down, overwhelmed by new ideas, new ways of thinking... at that point allowing the thinker to have their way, hurting or leaving them.

259. If you are super-talented, people want to know how tough you are. If you are tough that's all people want to know about you.

260. Emotional leadership will only take you so far. Strategic planning will sustain you for the rest of your life.

261. So many of us are so proficient at getting attention but keeping it is where we fall apart.

262. Those that are set in their ways are set to be alone with their ways.

263. When we desire something so badly, we can't rationally think or see straight. We hear and see truths other than how they are said or presented to us.

264. You can't be unappreciative of or wear out your support system. It's the hand that feeds you. If you don't eat, you die.

265. Before entering a relationship, first learn how to inspire others and accept inspiration.

266. What makes a great relationship is when the two know how to inspire one another.

267. People say "You just have to figure me out". All that means is "I want things my way or I'm going to be difficult."

268. Some people claim they want an opportunity to advance yet when presented with the opportunity they are always too busy with excuses as if their excuses are just as admirable as the opportunity.

269. I know people that give quick readymade answers to every unique opportunity. Then I realize they're just trying to avoid thinking.

270. Those that want control and order in every aspect of everybody's lives around them are really insecure and believe that's the only way to keep their own sanity.

271. If you just examine those that purposely take the joy out of others' lives, those individuals have no joy in theirs. Taking joy is their joy.

272. Some people think that keeping busy is living. That's like a manager keeping employees busy by having

them pretend to be cleaning when all of the cleaning has been done.

273. Most of us only know how to behave as we were taught. And if we had bad teachers, we have bad behavior and don't know it. We only know we have the same problems as our teachers.

274. An employee answering important questions when the owner or boss is not around is like a young child answering important questions when their parents aren't around.

275. When someone you care about is passionate and extends their hand by offering sentimental gifts or favors you don't think are important yet they are harmless... if you reject, minimize or criticize them, chances are that person will eventually stop extending anything to you even the things you do care about.

276. When you don't think what others are doing is important enough for you, don't be upset when others don't care what you're doing.

277. Wait for adversity before you commit. Insecurities rise as soon as circumstances don't go in the favor of the insecure person.

278. When you're not afraid anymore, you've conquered the illusion others have created for you or you have created for yourself.

279. So many people volunteer to help those that are talented and the talented wind up carrying the volunteers. That's the volunteer's game.

280. People want you to be afraid of what and who they're afraid of.

281. If we all decided today, right now, we want to be the most influential people ever, we could. Perception is power.

282. A friend places his kids in unhealthy environments expecting them to thrive but they don't. The unhealthy environments are convenient.

283. I'm always surprised when the smartest people in their fields of expertise can't make the simplest decisions in their personal lives.

284. What most unsuccessful people see as obstacles, successful people hurdle over or through. You don't have time to sit back and think about obstacles. You have to be conditioned to never see them as deterrents.

285. Those that think faster and more accurately than most will be ostracized and criticized until the rest of the people catch-up with that person's way

of thinking. In the meantime, quick accurate thinkers should keep their ideas to themselves and just leave others behind and only reveal their ideas when it is not detrimental to their ability to capitalize on their own brilliance.

286. It's hard to be around people that allow themselves to be misused and abused. After a while they expect you to take the abuse too. But then they turn on you saying things like, "You think you're better than me?" No, I just don't allow others to treat me like that. I have more self-worth and self-pride.

287. Being intelligent is not only knowing your next few moves but everybody else's next move.

288. You can live through others but you can't make those others do the things you think they should be doing. Those things may only make you happy and others bored or miserable.

289. When you realize the people you're dealing with are acting, take them off script into a subject they know nothing about... even you may not

know the subject, but if you are intelligent, the subject shouldn't matter. It's the natural curiosity you're looking for. Actors will pretend until they get you emotionally involved with their characters. After that, they confess they were only acting and they're insecure, confused and intimidated by original thinkers like you.

290. I hear people always say "I can't wait that long". But when that time passes and they're in the same place. They could've waited.

291. People fail because - at best - most of us are only familiar with what we know. When the pressure is on, what do we really know?

292. Religion gives hope to the poor that they will someday prosper and religion gives hope to the rich that the poor will not make it.

293. Reasonable and unreasonable is determined by the person who cares the least.

294. Placing our children into the hands of incompetent others is like placing expensive sport cars in the hands of demolition derby drivers.

295. I don't like or trust people that don't know the good things they have until they lose them or have to be constantly told by others about their blessings.

296. Help is all around us but we don't see it because what's in our minds is much greater.

297. Users want you to believe in them more than they want you to believe in yourself.

298. Those that hate you, hate that you don't acknowledge them as much as they do you.

299. Some people complain so much about everything that you don't know what to care about with them anymore.

300. We are conditioned to respect and believe those that bring us poverty as opposed to those that bring us wealth.

301. Don't pride yourself in fighting little bitty daily victories then shy away when it comes to important fights.

302. How the least influential of a race is treated by another determines race relations.

303. Many times you reach out to help others but they somehow misinterpret it as you needing them.

304. When I'm out and about, I see poverty of all races. So why is there racial prejudice again?

305. Correcting historical lies is not creating racial divide. The original historical lies did that.

306. When others seek your advice, most times they just want only what

they want to hear or what they already know.

307. Some have narrow perspectives as if what they see is the only valid solution, form or way of being. Life and the world is much bigger than that.

308. Strangers expect you to fight with them about things you only fight with loved ones over.

309. Most kids don't realize their lives are interesting. Most kids don't realize

their brains have the capacity to upload endless amounts of information like a computer. The brain is smarter than any computer.

310. With or without you, life always moves forward. Don't be like death.

311. In every relationship, you have to understand your worth or leverage to understand what you deserve and what to expect.

312. People think because they're talented, those that are not talented owe them in helping get their talent to the world. Foolish. Exploiting talent is others talent. That's how they make a living. Why else should they help you then?

313. Before you criticize what others are doing, can you do it better? Can you do it all? If not then how do you know what it takes? Because you've seen it done many times before? Is that how you determine your decision making based on what you know or have seen? Everything new has never been done before.

314. Those that say you can't achieve success or try to talk you out of it will actually get angry if you succeed without them.

315. If someone has the talent, it's not their talent that you want to work on. You want to fix their mind.

316. An incompetent teacher or coach in an incompetent environment goes unnoticed but not in a competent environment.

317. Most artists don't realize their art will be used by others to sell something else.

318. If you want to get to know someone, observe that person's behavior in a competitive environment, that'll tell you all you need to know about that person.

319. People have short memories when it's something bad or crazy they did. But when it's something others have done to them, they never forget.

320. All people are going to die anyway. So why are you taking this so seriously? You really think you're different? You know you're not going to be able to take that stuff you're working so hard for with you when you die. And those you leave it to, don't care that much about that stuff. They're just going to sell it and blow it on what they want.

321. Pros can tell if you're an amateur or a pro by the questions you ask or don't ask.

322. The people that are delaying everything don't have the freedom to move.

323. Those you don't need, make them think you need them, then watch how badly they treat you.

324. If the audience doesn't get it, it's not the audience. It's you. If individuals don't get it, who cares? Keep doing you.

325. Most of our manifested dreams are right in front of our faces but we

can't see them because they don't look like what's in our heads.

326. I meet many kids that are overwhelmed by opportunities, then when I meet their parents, I understand where their fears are coming from.

327. I don't mind you scrutinizing me but afterwards it'll be my turn to do the same to you. Don't be offended.

328. If people try to swindle you on things you know, imagine what they'll try on things you don't know.

329. Be careful who you ask to step up their game. They may leave you behind.

330. Unfortunately, most people only hear when others are angry at them and don't care anymore.

331. Overprotective parents produce children that make life decisions that are not well thought out.

332. Hanging around a super-intelligent person will either elevate or destroy you.

333. When you have a vision or a dream to accomplish, go as far as you can with it alone. Hopefully, that's to completion.

334. Your doubts about me won't stop me. I was just giving you the opportunity so that later you can't say you didn't know.

335. People get upset when you accept them for who they are rather than for who they want you to think they are.

336. The ones that are listened to the least in the beginning are the ones that usually have to hear about the big mess in the end.

337. When you find something special, you have to know or learn what to do with it before you make a move on it or risk losing, damaging or destroying it.

338. Most people fail because they're too good or too busy to do the minor, tedious, necessary things.

339. Marriage is a mentality. Reasons for successful marriages all depend on the two individuals' ways of thinking. Some people can be happy and one conversation with an outsider can turn that person's happiness to sadness. If love and trust is part of their agreement then so be it. Some marriages survive when the two have certain understandings that may not be considered healthy from society's point

of view of what an ideal marriage should be, but it can, nevertheless, survive. Many loveless marriages survive. Trust is a sense of being accepting of the other's quirkiness, odd habits or different ways of thinking.

340. Before you consider marriage, while you're dating that person, you have to pledge that person and be willing to be pledged. You have to take that person to their dark side and have to be willing to show yours. If after seeing and revealing the essence of one another then consider marriage. But you can't stop there. You have to then pledge one another's families, friends

and attachments to their past. Are they healthy? After going through all of this, chances are you won't marry that person. But if your game is tight enough, the other person will do it. That person will do anything you ask. If you are really secure within yourself, you'll do it. And if for nothing else, in the end, if it doesn't work out, you both will learn deep truths about yourselves.

341. You have to go after your dream as if no one will ever help and everyone is against you. The trick is you can't let anyone know you think this way.

342. Don't be the one holding up your team because you're trying to understand everything. That's why you have a team.

343. People defend evil, incompetence, thievery when they're benefitting. But when they're negatively affected, they suddenly develop a conscious.

344. Traditions are changed as new construction is changed. Everybody loves new construction; however, when you change tradition, you disconnect from the past and you get a new tradition with a new agenda.

345. Some people I thought were the most sane do really crazy things to keep their sanity.

346. Some people get strong and independent mixed up with wrong and independent.

347. Being broke kept me out of trouble. I couldn't afford to do anything bad. I had friends with money and their parents would pay their way out of trouble. If I got into trouble, I was just broke.

348. "What's in it for me?" is a question we hate to hear but love to give.

349. No matter how sophisticated we become, life is simple: companionship and family.

350. People actually believe that because God accepts them with all of their flaws and weaknesses that people should too.

351. I have a friend that's lucky. I work with him. I do my job and never question him because he's lucky. I always benefit.

352. I will never understand the people that believe it is good to hold down talented people - especially kids - in order to keep them from getting the "big head." Who are you promoting then?

353. All weaknesses aren't created equal. Neither are strengths.

354. People think just because they argue with you they are displaying intellectualism. It's only intellectual if you actually introduce a new perspective. If you're just repeating something you've heard, you're only being annoying.

355. Honesty is only good if it's helpful. The result of honesty sometimes can be worse than dishonesty.

356. Most women love babies. Therefore, a weak man's tactic to win a woman's affection that has that affinity towards children is to act childish.

357. The healthy food we eat when we're sick should be the food we eat all the time.

358. People will do their best to stop you from achieving your goal for whatever reason. But when they realize they cannot stop you, they'll pretend to be your biggest supporter. That is until they see you slipping.

359. Most times, you need to keep your new, undeveloped, interesting thoughts and ideas to yourself because

they will only be torn down simply out of ignorance or envy.

360. If you seek counsel from those that have experience in your dilemma, don't desire the counselor to feel your pain but only help you through your dilemma.

361. Naïveté is cute in a new relationship. But if the person continues to be naive and you commit to that person, you'll suffer.

362. Don't place your children in a punishment/reward environment. That's how you train slaves. Place them in a discipline/reward environment.

363. If you're around people that are not used to winning, even small victories can overwhelm them.

364. Sometimes we stick around too long in a place we've outgrown. Take those opportunities in between those years and build your own business. If you're bigger than your job, then act like it.

365. If you feel inferior, you're not the only one brainwashed. The person that feels superior is brainwashed too.

366. Certain lessons you can't learn by trial and error. You can't learn that jumping off a cliff will kill you by jumping off a cliff.

367. It's a matter of 'do we believe what actually happened' or what we were told happened?

368. As a comedian, you make a living observing others. Once famous, others observe you. It's no fun when you are the one being observed, especially if the persona you present on stage is not who you are offstage.

369. Love is accepting another's flaws still knowing that person won't accept yours.

370. Most people support each other's bad ideas, foolishness and sometimes ignorance because they want the same support in return.

371. The music I exposed my daughter to as a child she has returned to as an adult.

372. Genius is the ability to find the line not to cross and dance with it to spellbound admirers.

373. Thieves are trying to figure out whose side you're on, theirs or yours.

374. Most people never look inside of themselves because they believe the answers couldn't possibly be there.

375. Your real history doesn't match the fake education you were given.

376. If you are prepared, the doubt is not in yourself. It is in the unknown. And no one can do anything about the unknown. So why doubt?

377. If you truly find your history, you won't have to find God. You will know God.

378. The more you try to prove how important you are, it's more likely you will prove the opposite. Just be you.

379. Most people will waste your time supplying you with plenty of questions but never any answers.

380. Stubborn people get angry at why you didn't talk some sense into them

back then when they were making fools of themselves.

380. You just can't spring new information on people without first preparing their minds to receive it. They'll turn on you and may even become violent.

381. Sometimes you try to warn people of danger yet they choose not to take your warning so they proceed anyway resulting in disaster. Then you realize they didn't listen to you because they don't respect you or your advice.

382. Instead of striving for perfection, most people strive for the illusion of perfection.

383. People are afraid of truth that liberates them.

384. At times we are faced with tasks we dread. However, if we neglect them, we risk becoming controlled by those that gladly took on our tasks.

385. As a child never receiving a man's perspective, I realize so much of my life has been dedicated to catching up. Had I a smart, intelligent man's perspective, would my life have been more like my son's? His advantages are so much more expanded and time is not wasted deciding what is and what isn't. Unless wasted time was a part of my journey to discover what to pass on to my son.

386. You can't be too radical around people with plush lifestyles or those that want one. They'll sabotage you, rat you out, destroy you.

387. Some people feel the best way for them to catch up to you is to hate you.

388. When you stop in the moment to admire it, sometimes you lose the moment.

389. People want you to believe the lies they've learned because they've dedicated their lives to those lies.

390. The "ones that got away" were the lucky ones.

391. Lies are important. They motivate the masses. The truth is important too. It gets speakers of truth killed or eliminated.

392. How smart or intelligent you are is determined by how quickly you can unlearn ignorance.

393. Those slightly or grossly behind developmentally in relationships never know it until they are old and alone and sometimes not even then.

394. Remember, everybody's approaching a situation from their limited perspective.

395. Those that label themselves 'superior' seem to get sick, old and sometimes die at very young ages just like everybody else.

396. To be radically unique you can't take a conventional route. The conventional routes available are those for the obedient.

397. Being in the presence of very smart or brilliant people brings a lot of pressure unless you are humble then you know who and what you are. That in itself is very smart and brilliant.

398. When perpetrators of crime ask their victims to compromise, they are really saying, "Let me keep my ill-gotten gains and let's start anew."

399. Limiting impulsiveness and vices hopefully gauges maturity. If not, we're wasting many adventurous opportunities in our lives.

400. When enthusiasm is there but the plan's not quite solidified, don't allow others to kill your enthusiasm with their technicalities and fear.

401. Most people suffer from "I know failure happened to others but it won't happen to me" syndrome.

402. Deal with most adults like you would an unreasonable spoiled child.

403. While teaching, I had to meet every student where they were (even in a class of 20 plus) to find their motivation. If they had none, which most did not, I knew I had a clean slate to deal with. If the student had a motivation, I had to be creative and point that student in the right direction. He or she would find their way using me only as a guide to warn them of possibly wasted avenues.

404. Most people believe the best way for them to win is to constantly lose in order to gain experience.

405. The government is powerless over the people when people come together. But we only seem to come together during disasters or crises.

406. The promise of wealth keeps the poor loyal.

407. When you discover who you are inside, you realize how alone you are.

408. Yesterday's words cannot satisfy the hunger pain of tomorrow's new dilemma.

409. Don't get stuck on luck.

410. Success depends on the goal that's set. Failure depends on one's lack of understanding of that goal.

411. If a stranger can be corrected or conscience can be raised of misjudgment, misinterpretation, ignorance or prejudice, maybe someone else can be spared.

412. One of my main responsibilities is to remind our children of their mother's importance to them and how her needs trump theirs. I think the woman should do the same for her man. Collectively, the children will then receive the best of both parents and understand it.

413. If this world operated on intelligence, there'd be no wars.

414. We scramble to salvage the opportunity we pass on only when we see someone else seize that opportunity.

415. Those that perpetuate violence know the psychological damage it can do. That's why they're afraid when you threaten to retaliate.

416. We resist change because it might be to somebody else's advantage.

417. Great writing speaks in code to the intelligent.

418. If winning requires eliminating the illusion of cool, many prefer to lose.

419. Your power and importance are useless if you die and take them to the grave with you.

420. How does justice for me infringe upon your freedom? Unless you mean, your freedom depends on injustice against me.

421. Just remember everybody in front of you won't be there someday. They'll be behind you or gone.

422. Those that don't or have never supported you won't support you, regardless of how impressive you are.

423. Most times, the people that support you aren't the people you want to support you. And most people turn their backs on their supporters.

424. The time to fight for your rights is when your rights are not being violated.

425. When my daughter wears her hair natural, she becomes bored with it.

When she straightens her hair, days later, she becomes frustrated.

426. The mind is powerful and vulnerable all at the same time.

427. Have a great upside if you want people to put up with your downside.

428. Most don't know they have fragmented souls unless they luck up someday and feel what it's like to be whole.

429. Most people's success is hampered by having too little or too much.

430. We are hampered when we rely on others to eliminate the thinking needed for ourselves.

431. There are certain givens in life, routines we must master so that when pressure arises, we don't have to think about the routines.

432. There's a natural inclination for many to prove others wrong. However,

we take it too far when we try to disprove common sense.

433. Others assume you see the same value they see and you assume others see the same value as you. Either ask up front or be surprised later.

434. You can believe what you want but in the end it all comes down to might.

435. I teach my son how to survive in a room full of females. I give him subtle

nods of approval or disapproval then later explain the whys.

436. My son's learning the friends he chooses aren't always his real friends. Real friends are those that always want the best for him.

437. Marriage to some is an unthinkable achievement like winning the mega lotto or becoming an instant star. And once married, they behave like divas.

438. When prayers are needed, people send money. When money is needed, people send prayers.

439. People connect themselves permanently to great moments but then when those great moments have long passed, they become chains.

440. Warning shots sound negative.

441. People try to make reality opinion and deem it negative.

442. If I write what I like, it's easier. If I write what others want me to, it's hard.

443. Life happens with you or without you.

444. People want lies. Without lies, what is love?

445. Don't chase the dollars. Catch the opportunities.

446. Love is an action word.

447. To accept weaknesses in yourself or others is to accept the burdens that the come with those weaknesses.

448. Most places where there's poverty and lack of higher education, there is a lack of business sense and how the outside world actually operates. Hope is the biggest element of that environment; it is usually in the form of religion or motivational speakers. The middle class too are busy trying not to fall into that poor category but are only a financial mishap or two away from poverty. The rich are busy managing the middle class. The wealthy are busy enslaving the poor.

449. This is where money helps. Pay to remove those that don't like you or remove yourself?

450. If you're not and don't look like you're in shape, don't try to sell health products. Apparently, they do not work.

451. You have to prepare your mind for new, different, radical truths. Or like most, spend your life parroting other people's truths.

452. Today's society doesn't want children to fear their parents. Society wants parents to fear their children so that the children will be prime for prison.

453. Power is in the mystical. Take away the mystical and others have no power over you.

454. Those that say 'money is not important' or 'it's just money' have none and want yours.

455. In every situation, most are looking for one word, one phrase to hold on to. And that's their truth.

456. People want your help but they want you to prove you are worthy enough before you help them.

457. It's a waste helping you find solutions if you are comfortable being lost.

458. How you negotiate with a known thief, criminal or murderer is how you negotiate with the powers that be.

459. Some have great minds and terrible hearts. Others have great hearts and terrible minds. Either is a weak friend.

460. Some of the most meaningful intellectual exchanges I've experienced have come by over nutritious meals. If fast food is the norm, everything else exchanged is probably on the level of fast food consumption.

461. If there's a choice between receiving great advice or a loan: advice lasts a lifetime while loans place you in debt paying off interest.

462. Most people have just never grown up. They want what they want not what they need. The only things that seem to teach the immature are old age or bad health. There are even immature old people so maybe it's just bad health.

463. The young have a limited amount of time to exploit their youth. But like many athletes past their prime, they hang on too long.

464. If you're not married or divorced, your observation is like a small business professor that has never owned their own business.

465. People try to nurture their children to be tough before the fight. No. Train or have them trained. Throw them into the fight. Nurture them after the fight.

466. Don't spend your life trying to achieve what people deem ultimate success. That may take you a lifetime to realize that achievement is empty.

467. Value is a collective agreement of the brainwashed.

468. People can tolerate good or bad people. It's the inconsistent people we can't tolerate.

469. People always say, "Trust me." If I don't trust myself, why would I trust you?

470. Fathers have to respect women in order to raise daughters, and mothers have to respect men in order to raise sons.

471. Business has its own religion. Every body of all backgrounds worships the same principles.

472. Most are only up for the challenge if it's convenient.

473. Humans have to adjust to nature not the other way around or nature will eliminate the problem.

474. Light is more practical. Without it, there is no shadow. Love makes no shadow. Love only makes light. When love dies there is only shadow.

475. If you're looking for love, it's simple. Love the one that wants to love you.

476. Many people have internal conflict with what they know is the right thing to do and what is wrong (wrong being what they simply want).

477. Many want others to see the beauty in their imperfections rather than their imperfections.

478. Most seek counseling after their mistakes.

479. Others will try to talk you out of the good things you are doing for yourself because they don't feel like changing or thinking.

480. Those that listen do learn. Those that have issues and only teach - never listen, never learn.

481. Those only interested in fighting - that's how they love.

482. You can't find peace with those that constantly question their own sanity.

483. When you can't hold another to their own laws, rules and regulations, that is injustice.

484. People will settle in life to live but will die before settling in love.

485. If we practiced visualizing the long term results and repercussions of our

daily decisions, we would make different decisions.

486. The truth shocks because most won't tell the truth.

487. Those that don't like you for thinking too much of yourself, don't think too much of themselves.

488. The best way to discipline is to set realistic standards that must be met. When those standards are achieved then apply the next level.

489. If you fill your wish chest with contradictions of love, you better put wheels and a handle on it because you'll be pulling that chest through life alone.

490. Like with depression, some have bouts of happiness. Their happiness changes. Then they have to readjust. Very few are pretty much happy with the same things their entire lives.

491. Sometimes we ask for things we know we'll never get. It soothes our

egos that no one could ever meet our desires. It allows us to smile in public.

492. People get nervous around people that can say "No" anytime and can walk away.

493. Others don't have a problem with you knowing the truth. That's not the issue. Voicing the truth is.

494. Once you acquire knowledge, methods or weapons used to oppress

you, those things will suddenly be discredited or banned.

495. No matter what you do, you will receive negative criticism from those that think they can do it better.

496. When mice frighten elephants, it's funny. When a herd of elephants frighten mice, it's not funny.

497. Sometimes others, life or a desperate situation leaves you with nothing else to do except win.

498. If you don't have time to learn life lessons while you're young, you'll have plenty of time to learn them when you're old.

499. If you never challenge others to think, you'll always have plenty of company but very few friends.

500. Classless people treat you the way they don't want to be treated.

To the reader:

Ever since I can remember I've always spoken my mind and as a result I've often found myself ostracized, called bad names or even punished by those in authority such as elders, my parents, older siblings or teachers. I was often accused of being a "smart mouthed" kid who thought he was better than everybody. I never thought I was better than everybody but I did think that as people we could always do better, whether treating one another better or urging others to think differently, especially if our current thoughts weren't making our lives better. Needless to say, I spent so much of my childhood isolated from others, wondering whether something was wrong with me or others. Every now and then, I'd find a kindred soul but that soul was usually an elderly person or (as my mother would say) some "touched" individual. I enjoyed their life lessons immensely but after a while, even I began avoiding them because the elderly would usually want me to do some physical work for them for no pay like clean up their houses, go to the store for them or just hang around them until they needed something done. As I got older I didn't mind helping and actually enjoyed it but as a young kid, I just wanted to either listen to a great story or lesson or simply play. As for the "touched" individuals I'd encounter, their ideas were always immersed in conspiracy theories. I really enjoyed those theories but those individuals would charge for those lessons, either they wanted your money or your food, which as a kid I had neither. So I'd move on to the next "touched" character. That's probably why I was always told I was different. I never knew at the time what that meant. Maybe I didn't know because I'm "touched." The words that came out of my mouth sounded normal to me, maybe because the voice inside of me was constantly talking and I'd gotten used to that voice. Later, I learned that voice was in all people and it's called intuition. That's a very smart voice. It tells you when you're doing right or wrong. It tells you when someone is nice or not. It tells you when danger is about to occur. I've listened to that voice all of my life and many times that voice contradicts what those in authority are telling you. Sometimes we become so afraid to go against those in authority that we begin to silence that voice inside of us. That voice is like a light. When we allow it to be put out, we are left with only darkness inside. But when we listen to that voice inside of us, we become strong and confident. That voice makes us curious. It makes us want to know more. It makes us want to seek truth, whatever that truth may be, whether it's our own truth or the truth of others. Either truth, once we know it and learn it, we become closer to universal truths, those things we understand without having to say aloud and when we hear or see those truths, it awakens in us that inner voice that has been talking to us all of our lives.

ABOUT THE AUTHOR

Professor Ray Grant has a Master of Fine Arts (MFA) in poetry from the University of Iowa's world-renowned Writers Workshop and he became a published poet while a student there. The U of I is also where he received his Bachelor of Arts (BA) in English. After leaving Iowa, he began a teaching career, teaching creative, screenplay and composition writing for 17 years at Tuskegee University, Spelman College and Morehouse College. While teaching at Spelman, a comedy club owner was visiting the campus and he and the young Professor struck up an amusing conversation. The comedy club owner invited The Professor to try his hand at standup comedy at his local Atlanta comedy club. In one year of failing and trying over and over again week after week to make the most hostile audiences laugh, he was discovered by a TV comedy scout and The Professor was selected to make his TV standup comedy performance debut on HBO in 1996. Since then, he's gone on to travel the world performing standup while continuing to teach. He also continued writing and performing poetry as well and made a TV appearance on TVOne's Verses & Flow. He met his wife, Paula, while performing standup at an Atlanta comedy club. Three years later they married and had two children, a girl, Rae, and a boy, Donovan.

www.ingramcontent.com/pod-product-compliance
Lightning Source LLC
Chambersburg PA
CBHW060750050426
42449CB00008B/1352